AF492656

also by Matt Schatz

Shoes Last Longer in LA

Dramaturgatory
Poems For Theater People

By Matt Schatz

Kung Fu Treachery Press

Rancho Cucamonga, California

Copyright © Matt Schatz, 2026

First Edition: 1 3 5 7 9 10 8 6 4 2

ISBN: 979-8-89975-045-8

LCCN: 2026939217

Cover and title page image: Matt Schatz

Acknowledgments

Some of these poems have appeared, or will appear, in *Light* and *J Journal*, and on the author's social media pages, where they've been liked, loved, and shared by some of the best theater people around.

An earlier, shorter boutique edition of *Dramaturgatory* was published by Bala Court Press (2025) in a limited, signed, and numbered run.

Table of Contents

ACT I

ACT II

ACT III

ACT IV

ACT V

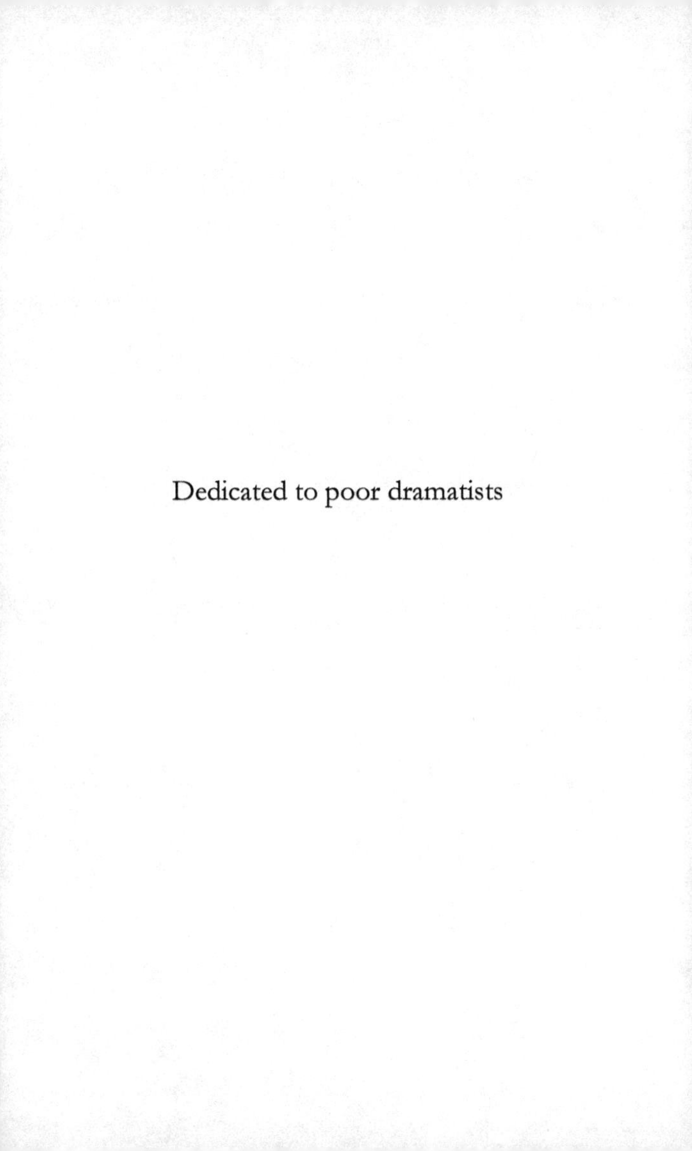

Dedicated to poor dramatists

The Drama Bug

While getting my M.F.A.
At CMU,
They put me on a student play
To do run crew.
They say when you do a show,
Your skin tingles.
And that's why I did not know
I had shingles.

Welcome to Dramaworld

There's a ride called "The Pause,"
In a section called "Pinterville."
It's over—applause!
But it's only the interval.

In the Youngblood Playwrights' Group at Ensemble Studio Theatre

A now very famous playwright
Asked me to be in her play.
I thought it was a joke—
Her name is (redacted).
Her lines I couldn't say right.
I'm embarrassed to this day.
She liked the way I spoke,
But hated when I acted.

The Antagonist

In his imaginary playwriting course,
He despised taking students to task.
But his most annoying imaginary student
Had the audacity to ask:
"Why on earth is it playwright?
What are the G and H doing there?"
"Playwrights are like shipwrights—
They craft something that takes you
    somewhere."
"Then why isn't it playwriting?"
The pain in the ass replied.
"I don't know," he said,
As he sat and stared outside.

The Hypocrite

Oxford shirt,
And Oxford shoes,
The Oxford School of Drama.
Yet you assert
That you refuse
To use the Oxford comma.

The Dramaturg

Her theater has hoards
Of awards.
She never gives notes—
She gives chords.

The Dramatist

She felt like a fraud,
'Cause she made it all up.
Would they even applaud?
But they ate it all up.
And she was so awed
When, after the show,
There was only one question:
"How did you know?"

True Crime

Sweet Jesus
And holy hell:
Oedipus was not Sophocles'
Story to tell.

The Work of Art

Thank God for the big Broadway show!
Such a difficult artform to master.
They say if it doesn't play in Peoria,
It may never sell out the Belasco.
If one element doesn't quite go,
The whole thing can be a disaster.
But on the train back to Astoria,
They were glad it was just a fiasco.

Advice for Playwrights

Apply to the thing.
You won't get it.
But that's one more place
You don't have to credit.

Playwright's Note

I never know quite what to say when
They ask, "What's your play about?"
But I've not felt this way about a play
Since the last play I felt this way about.

So Many Stories Stay on the Page

After the emerging stage,
Some playwrights have
The nerve to age.

ACT II

Regional Theater Pro Tip

If your play's not reducible
To a fun signature drink,
It's not unproducible—
But you'd be wise to think
Before you waste your ink.

My Pitch to Replace Jesse Green

Dear people of The New York Times:
I will write reviews with rhymes.

I won't say what I didn't care for;
That is not what I'll be there for.

My job will be to simply say
That anybody makes a play

Is such a stupid miracle.
And as a bonus, I'll be lyrical.

Giving Tuesday

So many theaters wrote me today
But it wasn't to tell me they're doing my play

Seeking Opportunities For:

Descending playwrights,
Sad-ending playwrights,
Gray-bearded empiricists,
Declining playwrights,
Resigning playwrights,
And disappearing lyricists.
Receding playwrights,
Beg-pleading playwrights,
Poem-posting posers,
Submerging playwrights,
Diverging playwrights,
And decomposed composers.

The Retiree

He's got a great idea for a play.
He needs a guy like you to make it funny.
If you can help him write it, he will pay—
He's got a lot of friends with tons of
     money.

The Actor

He's never had a callback,
And never had a fallback.
He's regretted each endeavor,
But would never take it all back.

The Performer

He sat on a catapult
And got shot into knives.
It had gotten so difficult;
It was giving him hives.
The pay was quite low.
The work was unsteady.
With one show to go,
He missed it already.

The Work Trip

Out of town for a theater fest,
He's grateful for the break.
But without children
    disturbing his rest,
He's awake.

Keep Your Mouth Shut

I had a hand in your success,
And you have said so in the press!
You even mention me by name!
I only have myself to blame.

A Wicked Troll on Facebook

I am a writer, my name is Matt Schatz.
I wrote a true crime musical with
    too much mirth.
And some lawyer in Colorado
    named Jonathan Datz
Vowed to hunt me to the ends of
    the Earth.

The Comments Have Been
Turned Off

Never ask for feedback.
Feedback is for schmendriks.
No one's made art from it—
Except for Jimi Hendrix.

Playwrights Union

Writing a screenplay at a coffee shop
Is hoary and whorey
But writing a stage play at a coffee shop
Is a whole nother story

Corporate Art

I once wrote an entire play
In a Capital One Café

Guy in Your Playwriting Group

While at Yale
Became a macher
Alpha male
w/ beta blocker

Diminishing Returns

A two-person show
Is more producible than a three.
And a one-person show
Is more producible than a two.
And a no-person show
Is one no person wants to see—
Thanks to that New York Times review.

Not Getting the Playwriting Professor Job

You won't get to show off every ability,
Or answer every question you
  prepared for,
But you get to see the brand-
  new daycare facility,
Where your toddler will never
  get to be cared for.

Double Major: Theater/ Mathematics

He'd count his blessings
But it's hard for him to count
Such a small amount

The Names May Be the Same But

I didn't plagiarize your play
If this is what is being claimed.
I'll send a PDF your way
Where the changes have been named.

Dr. Titleman

Don't like the names of my plays?
See how you feel in a couple of days.

ACT III

Stephen Sondheim Said

"Poetry is an art of compression,
Lyrics of expansion."
Poets live inside confession;
Lyricists, a mansion.

Ephen Stephen

Life is something to be endured.
Life is a celebration of endurance.
He got a rejection from the Fred Ebb Award,
But he got an acceptance from
    unemployment insurance.

Elevator Pitch

A revival of Cats where they're not
  cats!
A revival of Starlight Express where
  they're not trains!
Both with a new book by Matt Schatz!
Every song remains!

Ballad of the Three-Chord
Musical Theater Composer

I've won more than one
Songwriting award.
Here's some advice, son:
They don't pay by the chord.

I'm Just Like Mozart

But only when it comes to finances.
Things can get a little hairy.
But you gotta take the finest chances—
When you're your own worst Salieri.

Richard Linklater's Blue Moon

Larry Hart was a New York Jew.
Richard Rodgers was one too.
But Ethan Hawke and Andrew Scott
Are not.

Finally Watching Blue Moon on the Way to and from a Musical Workshop

Dare to be like Larry Hart.
Care about your fate.
Live to make immortal art,
And die at forty-eight.

Artificial Intelligence

I will skip Bill and Ted in Godot.
You know I'm not much for plays.
But I'll take my self-driving auto
To see Tilly Norwood in Happy Days.

Ernest Hemingway Said

"Write hard and clear
About what hurts."
For hours I've been sitting here,
And so my butt hurts.

Another Theater Poem

I thought I'd seen Marjorie Prime.
Turns out that was Maple and Vine.
I know that this is a false rhyme,
But wait till you read the last line!

ACT IV

Don't Worry, My Friend

There's always a lot to dismay.
There's always so much on your plate.
But each time you say your play
    went OK,
I know that it really went great.

The Kennedy Center
Cannot Hold

Think about the oath you took
When you raised your hand.
Anyone who's banned a book
Shouldn't book a band.

Denomination

The theater is your temple,
But temple is a theater too.
You're an observant playwright,
And a less-than-fervent Jew.
You never want to go to either;
You're mostly happy when you do.

Poem for Milan Stitt

(1941–2009, Chair of Dramatic Writing,
Carnegie Mellon University)

I knew this was an impossible vocation,
But he made me believe I had a
    fighting chance.
He'd answer the door without hesitation—
Or pants.

Some Old Guy I Met After Winning an Award

He said he had read my musical,
And predicted that I would do well.
He asked me where my family
    summered:
"Where we wintered, sprang,
    and fell."

The Only Thing You Really Need to Know

He was going to wait
Until she was older,
But he rubbed his eyes
And gazed into hers—
Two translucent opals.
His two-year-old date
Nodded as he told her,
Much to his surprise,
That he vastly prefers
Zero Mostel's Tevye
To Topol's.

Admission Statement

Remember that Valentine's Day?
Where I sent you all those po'ms,
Then I broke my tooth on one of
    those heart mints?
Being an artist is a pain in the tooth
That never, ever eases up.
This is a roundabout way for me
    to say
There are no creative homes;
There are only creative apartments.
And it's the landlords, not the artists,
Who tell you the truth—
And the truth is, baby,
The lease is up.

Day One of My Writing Class

It's all one big haiku;
Account for every syllable.
Lie a lot; be true.
All your darlings: killable.

The Writer

These bitter little bites
Are baked on premises.
I wouldn't wish my friendship
On my greatest nemesis.

An Allergic Reaction to Success

At the opening night party,
I wanted something hearty.
I got the calamari,
And for that, I am sorry.

Bittersweet Sympathies

Her play's unproduced and she's peeved—
It's a feeling that persists.
But at least she doesn't feel aggrieved
When left off year-end lists.

ACT V

Inciting Incident

I decided to fight the dragon.
I'm the weakest; he's the dragonest.
It was a false decision—
It's why I'm the protagonist.

Where the Sidewalk Ends

(After Silverstein)

That poem always filled me with wonder,
But I think about the title on long
    walks, when
The day gets gray and the sky cries
    thunder,
And the concrete quickly terminates.
    And then
I find myself at a terrible impasse:
To imperil myself on the side of
    the road,
Or crunch through newly wet and
    overgrown grass,
Shouldering a cold and heavy load.

And suddenly, this Sunday stroller
    is ill at ease.
There is a gravity that pushes
    instead of pulls.
Ahead—where once were many
    possibilities—
Is now a street replete with
    obstacles.

Credo

Uplift other artists
(This business is luck)
Over the guardrails
And into a truck.

The Failure

He takes a big swing
At every little thing

All of My Best Musical
Theater Songs

The second song I wrote,
And the praise was universal—
For after every reading
The audience left whistling.
But someone gave a note,
So we cut it in rehearsal.
The musical's still bleeding;
The author is still bristling.

A Life in the Theater,
Or I Once Sold Snickerdoodles
in the Lobby of Philadelphia's
Arden Theatre Company

You start out selling concessions.
You end up making them.

The Human Factor

The GPS voice mispronounces
    street names.
The AI artist always mangles hands.
But after the play, an audience
    member exclaims:
Someone somewhere out there
    understands.

This project was made possible, in part, by generous support from the Osage Arts Community.

Osage Arts Community provides temporary time, space and support for the creation of new artistic works in a retreat format, serving creative people of all kinds — visual artists, composers, poets, fiction and nonfiction writers. Located on a 152-acre farm in an isolated rural mountainside setting in Central Missouri and bordered by ¾ of a mile of the Gasconade River, OAC provides residencies to those working alone, as well as welcoming collaborative teams, offering living space and workspace in a country environment to emerging and mid-career artists. For more information, visit us at www.osageac.org